Mangrove Swamps

Kimberley Jane Pryor

Smart Apple Media

This edition first published in 2008 in the United States of America by Smart Apple Media.
All rights reserved. No part of this book may be reproduced in any form or by any means without written permission from the publisher.

Smart Apple Media
2140 Howard Drive West
North Mankato, Minnesota 56003

First published in 2007 by
MACMILLAN EDUCATION AUSTRALIA PTY LTD
627 Chapel Street, South Yarra, Australia 3141

Visit our Web site at www.macmillan.com.au or go directly to www.macmillanlibrary.com.au

Associated companies and representatives throughout the world.

Copyright © Kimberley Jane Pryor 2007

Library of Congress Cataloging-in-Publication Data

Pryor, Kimberley Jane.
  Mangrove swamps / by Kimberley Jane Pryor.
    p. cm. — (Wonders of the sea)
  Includes index.
  ISBN 978-1-59920-138-2
  1. Mangrove ecology—Juvenile literature. 2. Mangrove swamps—Juvenile literature. I. Title.

  QH541.5.M27P79 2007
  577.69'8—dc22

                                                        2007004781

Edited by Erin Richards
Text and cover design by Christine Deering
Page layout by Domenic Lauricella
Photo research by Legend Images

Printed in U.S.

Acknowledgements
The author and the publisher are grateful to the following for permission to reproduce copyright material:

Cover photograph: Fish swimming in a mangrove swamp courtesy of Joe Stancampiano/National Geographic/Getty Images.

© Images&Stories/Alamy, p. 13 (bottom); Doug Perrine/AUSCAPE, p. 12 (bottom); Keith Davey, pp. 3, 15, 27 (left); Dreamstime, pp. 13 (top), 30; futureofcairns.net, p. 17; Joe Stancampiano/National Geographic/Getty Images, pp. 1, 11; Stuart Westmorland/Getty Images, p. 12 (top); © Greenpeace/Urrutia, p. 29; Grant Johnson, Bimini Biological Field Station, p. 22; Hans & Judy Beste/Lochman Transparencies, p. 5; Clay Bryce/Lochman Transparencies, pp. 10, 16, 25; Jiri Lochman/Lochman Transparencies, pp. 8, 14, 19, 26; Dr Stuart Miller/Lochman Transparencies, p. 27 (right); Col Roberts/Lochman Transparencies, p. 18; Jay Sarson/Lochman Transparencies, p. 6; G. Saueracker/Lochman Transparencies, p. 9; NASA Goddard Space Flight Center, p. 4; Jurgen Freund/naturepl.com, p. 20; Photolibrary.com/OSF/Tobias Bernhard, p. 21; Photolibrary.com/OSF/Mary Plage, p. 23; Photolibrary.com/Photo Researchers Inc, p. 24; Photolibrary.com/Alexis Rosenfeld/Science Photo Library, p. 7; Photolibrary.com/Superstock, Inc/Larry Prosor, p. 28.

While every care has been taken to trace and acknowledge copyright, the publisher tenders their apologies for any accidental infringement where copyright has proved untraceable. Where the attempt has been unsuccessful, the publisher welcomes information that would redress the situation.

For Nick, Thomas and Ashley
– Kimberley Jane Pryor

Contents

Glossary words

When a word is printed in **bold**, you can look up its meaning in the glossary on page 31.

The sea

The sea is a very large area of salty water.
It covers most of Earth's surface.

The blue part of Earth is the sea.

The sea has many different **habitats**. Mangrove swamps are habitats found where the sea meets the land.

Mangrove swamps are found in warm, shallow water.

Mangrove swamps

Mangrove swamps are areas where mangrove trees grow. When the **tide** is in, the roots of mangrove trees are covered with salty water.

Mangrove trees can grow in salty water.

Mangrove swamps are full of life. They provide food and shelter for many different plants and animals.

Fish shelter among the roots of mangrove trees.

Plants

Mangrove trees are plants that can grow in mud and survive in salty water. Mangrove trees often have no other plants growing beneath them.

Few plants can grow in the mud under mangrove trees.

Mangrove tree roots grow down from the trunk or stick up out of the mud. Small plants, called seaweed, sometimes grow on these roots.

Small seaweed grows on the roots of mangrove trees.

Seaweed

Animals

Many different animals live in mangrove swamps. At **low tide**, crabs and sea snails look for food on the mud.

Mud creepers search the mud for food.

At **high tide**, fish swim into mangrove swamps to feed.

Fish search among the mangrove roots for food.

Where animals live

In a mangrove swamp, each kind of animal has a special place to live.

Golden cownose rays are sometimes seen near the surface of the water.

Spiny lobsters live on the sea floor.

Yellow-crowned night herons search the mud for crabs to eat.

Gray angelfish swim among the roots of the mangroves.

Survival

To survive in a mangrove swamp, animals need to find and eat food. Mudskippers leave the water to look for food on the mud.

Special fins for skipping across the mud

Big eyes for looking for food

Mudskippers search for plants and small animals on the mud.

Animals also need to protect themselves from **predators**. Some use their colors and others use their body parts.

Hard plates that shut quickly when in danger

Barnacles use their hard plates to protect them from predators.

Small animals

Small animals live all over mangrove swamps.
Crabs scurry over the mud and climb the trunks
of mangrove trees.

Mangrove crabs have large claws.

Young prawns and shrimps search the water for rotting plants and animals to eat.

A pistol shrimp has one claw much bigger than the other.

Fish

Many young fish live in mangrove swamps because they find food there. They can also hide from predators under the mangrove roots.

Many young fish feed among the roots of mangrove trees.

Some fish leave mangrove swamps to live on coral reefs or in the open sea. Other fish stay near mangrove swamps their whole lives.

Some flounders live in the shallow water near mangrove swamps.

Some sharks swim into mangrove swamps to give birth to their young.

These lemon sharks were born in a mangrove swamp.

Archerfish knock the insects they eat off mangrove trees. They do this by spitting droplets of water at them.

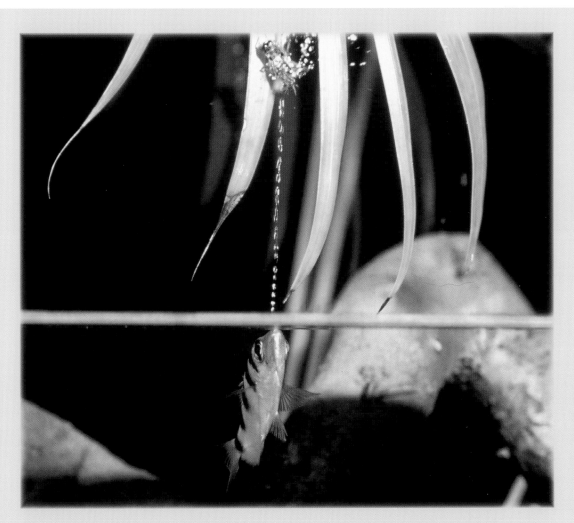

An archerfish can knock a fly off a leaf by spitting at it.

Living together

Animals often live together for protection. Some fish swim in a group, called a school. This makes it harder for a predator to choose and catch a fish.

A school of fish may hide under mangrove tree roots.

Some animals survive by living on plants. Oysters often attach themselves to mangrove tree roots. They get their food from the water when the tide comes in.

Mangrove tree roots keep oysters up out of the mud.

Food chain

Living things depend on other living things for food. This is called a food chain.

This is how a food chain works.

Plant food for ➤

This is a simple mangrove swamp food chain.

 food for ➤

Mangrove trees make their food using energy from the sun.

Plant-eating animal → food for → Animal-eating animal

Fallen, rotting leaves of mangrove trees are food for semaphore crabs.

Semaphore crabs are food for eastern curlews.

Threats to mangrove swamps

Mangrove swamps can be **threatened** by natural events, such as hurricanes. During these storms, wild winds break the branches of mangrove trees.

A hurricane can damage mangrove trees.

Mangrove swamps are also threatened by people who:

- allow oil to flow into mangrove swamps
- cut down mangrove trees
- trample the roots of mangrove trees

These shrimp farms were once a mangrove swamp.

Protecting mangrove swamps

We help protect mangrove swamps when we:

- stop pouring oil down sinks and drains
- stop cutting down mangrove trees
- build **boardwalks** to walk over mangrove
  tree roots

Boardwalks protect the roots of mangrove trees.

Glossary

boardwalks   paths that people can walk on so that they do not trample plants

habitats   places where plants or animals naturally grow or live

high tide   when the sea has moved toward the land

low tide   when the sea has moved away from the land

predators   animals that hunt, kill, and eat other animals

prey   animals that are killed and eaten by other animals

threatened   placed in danger

tide   the movement of the sea toward the land and away from the land

Index